DATE _____

TODAY'S PASSAGE                    PREACHER

NOTES
_____
_____
_____
_____
_____
_____
_____
_____
_____
_____
_____

PRAYER
_____
_____
_____
_____
_____
_____
_____
_____
_____
_____
_____
_____
_____
_____
_____

KEY VERSES

KEY POINTS

APPLICATION

# Prayer journal

DATE _____

TODAY'S PASSAGE          PREACHER          SERMON TOPIC

NOTES

KEY VERSES

PRAYER

KEY POINTS

APPLICATION

# Prayer journal

DATE

TODAY'S PASSAGE          PREACHER          SERMON TOPIC

NOTES

KEY VERSES

PRAYER

KEY POINTS

APPLICATION

# Prayer journal

DATE _____

TODAY'S PASSAGE          PREACHER          SERMON TOPIC

NOTES
_____
_____
_____
_____
_____
_____
_____
_____
_____
_____
_____
_____
_____

PRAYER
_____
_____
_____
_____
_____
_____
_____
_____
_____
_____
_____
_____
_____
_____
_____

| KEY VERSES |
| --- |
|  |

| KEY POINTS |
| --- |
|  |

| APPLICATION |
| --- |
|  |

# Prayer journal

DATE _____

TODAY'S PASSAGE          PREACHER          SERMON TOPIC

NOTES
_____
_____
_____
_____
_____
_____
_____
_____
_____
_____
_____

PRAYER
_____
_____
_____
_____
_____
_____
_____
_____
_____
_____
_____
_____
_____
_____
_____
_____

KEY VERSES

KEY POINTS

APPLICATION

# Prayer journal

DATE _____

TODAY'S PASSAGE          PREACHER          SERMON TOPIC

NOTES
_____
_____
_____
_____
_____
_____
_____
_____
_____
_____
_____

PRAYER
_____
_____
_____
_____
_____
_____
_____
_____
_____
_____
_____
_____
_____
_____

| KEY VERSES |
| --- |
|  |

| KEY POINTS |
| --- |
|  |

| APPLICATION |
| --- |
|  |

# Prayer journal

DATE

TODAY'S PASSAGE          PREACHER          SERMON TOPIC

NOTES

KEY VERSES

PRAYER

KEY POINTS

APPLICATION

# Prayer journal

DATE _____

TODAY'S PASSAGE          PREACHER          SERMON TOPIC

NOTES
_____
_____
_____
_____
_____
_____
_____
_____
_____
_____
_____
_____

PRAYER
_____
_____
_____
_____
_____
_____
_____
_____
_____
_____
_____
_____
_____
_____

| KEY VERSES |
| --- |
|  |

| KEY POINTS |
| --- |
|  |

| APPLICATION |
| --- |
|  |

# Prayer journal

DATE _____

TODAY'S PASSAGE          PREACHER          SERMON TOPIC

NOTES
_____
_____
_____
_____
_____
_____
_____
_____
_____
_____
_____
_____
_____

| KEY VERSES |
| --- |
| |

PRAYER
_____
_____
_____
_____
_____
_____
_____
_____
_____
_____
_____
_____
_____
_____
_____
_____
_____
_____

| KEY POINTS |
| --- |
| |

| APPLICATION |
| --- |
| |

# Prayer journal

DATE _____

TODAY'S PASSAGE          PREACHER          SERMON TOPIC

NOTES
_____
_____
_____
_____
_____
_____
_____
_____
_____
_____

PRAYER
_____
_____
_____
_____
_____
_____
_____
_____
_____
_____
_____
_____
_____
_____
_____

KEY VERSES

KEY POINTS

APPLICATION

# Prayer journal

DATE

TODAY'S PASSAGE                    PREACHER                    SERMON TOPIC

NOTES

KEY VERSES

PRAYER

KEY POINTS

APPLICATION

# Prayer journal

DATE _____

TODAY'S PASSAGE          PREACHER          SERMON TOPIC

NOTES
_____
_____
_____
_____
_____
_____
_____
_____
_____
_____
_____

PRAYER
_____
_____
_____
_____
_____
_____
_____
_____
_____
_____
_____
_____
_____
_____

| KEY VERSES |
| --- |
|  |

| KEY POINTS |
| --- |
|  |

| APPLICATION |
| --- |
|  |

# Prayer journal

DATE

TODAY'S PASSAGE

PREACHER

SERMON TOPIC

NOTES

KEY VERSES

PRAYER

KEY POINTS

APPLICATION

# Prayer journal

DATE _____

TODAY'S PASSAGE          PREACHER          SERMON TOPIC

NOTES

_____
_____
_____
_____
_____
_____
_____
_____
_____
_____
_____
_____

PRAYER

_____
_____
_____
_____
_____
_____
_____
_____
_____
_____
_____
_____
_____
_____
_____

| KEY VERSES |
| --- |
| |

| KEY POINTS |
| --- |
| |

| APPLICATION |
| --- |
| |

# Prayer journal

DATE _____

TODAY'S PASSAGE          PREACHER          SERMON TOPIC

NOTES
_____
_____
_____
_____
_____
_____
_____
_____
_____
_____
_____
_____

| KEY VERSES |
| --- |
|  |

PRAYER
_____
_____
_____
_____
_____
_____
_____
_____

| KEY POINTS |
| --- |
|  |

_____
_____
_____
_____
_____
_____
_____
_____
_____

| APPLICATION |
| --- |
|  |

# Prayer journal

DATE _____

TODAY'S PASSAGE | PREACHER | SERMON TOPIC

NOTES
_____
_____
_____
_____
_____
_____
_____
_____
_____
_____
_____

PRAYER
_____
_____
_____
_____
_____
_____
_____
_____
_____
_____
_____
_____
_____
_____
_____

KEY VERSES

KEY POINTS

APPLICATION

# Prayer journal

DATE _____

TODAY'S PASSAGE          PREACHER                    SERMON TOPIC

NOTES
_____
_____
_____
_____
_____
_____
_____
_____
_____
_____
_____
_____
_____

PRAYER
_____
_____
_____
_____
_____
_____
_____
_____
_____
_____
_____
_____
_____
_____
_____

KEY VERSES

KEY POINTS

APPLICATION

# Prayer journal

DATE _____

TODAY'S PASSAGE          PREACHER          SERMON TOPIC

NOTES

KEY VERSES

PRAYER

KEY POINTS

APPLICATION

# Prayer journal

DATE

TODAY'S PASSAGE

PREACHER

SERMON TOPIC

NOTES

KEY VERSES

PRAYER

KEY POINTS

APPLICATION

# Prayer journal

DATE _____

TODAY'S PASSAGE          PREACHER          SERMON TOPIC

NOTES
_____
_____
_____
_____
_____
_____
_____
_____
_____
_____
_____

| KEY VERSES |
| --- |
|  |

PRAYER
_____
_____
_____
_____
_____
_____

| KEY POINTS |
| --- |
|  |

_____
_____
_____
_____
_____
_____
_____
_____
_____

| APPLICATION |
| --- |
|  |

# Prayer journal

DATE _____

TODAY'S PASSAGE          PREACHER          SERMON TOPIC

NOTES
_____
_____
_____
_____
_____
_____
_____
_____
_____
_____
_____
_____

| KEY VERSES |
|:---:|
|  |

PRAYER
_____
_____
_____
_____
_____
_____
_____
_____
_____
_____
_____
_____
_____
_____
_____
_____

| KEY POINTS |
|:---:|
|  |

| APPLICATION |
|:---:|
|  |

# Prayer journal

DATE _____

TODAY'S PASSAGE          PREACHER          SERMON TOPIC

NOTES
_____
_____
_____
_____
_____
_____
_____
_____
_____
_____
_____

PRAYER
_____
_____
_____
_____
_____
_____
_____
_____
_____
_____
_____
_____
_____
_____

KEY VERSES

KEY POINTS

APPLICATION

# Prayer journal

DATE _____

TODAY'S PASSAGE          PREACHER                    SERMON TOPIC

NOTES
_____
_____
_____
_____
_____
_____
_____
_____
_____
_____
_____

| KEY VERSES |
|:----------:|
|            |

PRAYER
_____
_____
_____
_____
_____
_____
_____

| KEY POINTS |
|:----------:|
|            |

_____
_____
_____
_____
_____
_____
_____
_____

| APPLICATION |
|:-----------:|
|             |

# Prayer journal

DATE _____

TODAY'S PASSAGE          PREACHER                    SERMON TOPIC

NOTES

_____

_____

_____

_____

_____

_____

_____

_____

_____

_____

_____

PRAYER

_____

_____

_____

_____

_____

_____

_____

_____

_____

_____

_____

_____

_____

| KEY VERSES |
| --- |
|  |

| KEY POINTS |
| --- |
|  |

| APPLICATION |
| --- |
|  |

DATE _____

# Prayer journal

TODAY'S PASSAGE _____   PREACHER _____   SERMON TOPIC _____

NOTES
_____
_____
_____
_____
_____
_____
_____
_____
_____
_____
_____

PRAYER
_____
_____
_____
_____
_____
_____
_____
_____
_____
_____
_____
_____
_____
_____
_____
_____

| KEY VERSES |
| --- |
|  |

| KEY POINTS |
| --- |
|  |

| APPLICATION |
| --- |
|  |

# Prayer journal

DATE _____

TODAY'S PASSAGE          PREACHER                    SERMON TOPIC

NOTES
_____
_____
_____
_____
_____
_____
_____
_____
_____
_____
_____

PRAYER
_____
_____
_____
_____
_____
_____
_____
_____
_____
_____
_____
_____
_____
_____
_____
_____

KEY VERSES

KEY POINTS

APPLICATION

# Prayer journal

DATE

TODAY'S PASSAGE          PREACHER          SERMON TOPIC

NOTES

KEY VERSES

PRAYER

KEY POINTS

APPLICATION

# Prayer journal

DATE _____

TODAY'S PASSAGE          PREACHER          SERMON TOPIC

NOTES
_____
_____
_____
_____
_____
_____
_____
_____
_____
_____
_____

PRAYER
_____
_____
_____
_____
_____
_____
_____
_____
_____
_____
_____
_____
_____
_____
_____

KEY VERSES

KEY POINTS

APPLICATION

# Prayer journal

DATE _____

TODAY'S PASSAGE          PREACHER          SERMON TOPIC

NOTES
_____
_____
_____
_____
_____
_____
_____
_____
_____
_____
_____

PRAYER
_____
_____
_____
_____
_____
_____
_____
_____
_____
_____
_____
_____
_____
_____
_____
_____

KEY VERSES

KEY POINTS

APPLICATION

# Prayer journal

DATE _____

TODAY'S PASSAGE          PREACHER          SERMON TOPIC

NOTES
_____
_____
_____
_____
_____
_____
_____
_____
_____
_____
_____
_____

PRAYER
_____
_____
_____
_____
_____
_____
_____
_____
_____
_____
_____
_____
_____
_____
_____
_____
_____

KEY VERSES

KEY POINTS

APPLICATION

# Prayer journal

DATE _____

TODAY'S PASSAGE          PREACHER          SERMON TOPIC

NOTES
_____
_____
_____
_____
_____
_____
_____
_____
_____
_____
_____

PRAYER
_____
_____
_____
_____
_____
_____
_____
_____
_____
_____
_____
_____
_____
_____
_____
_____
_____

KEY VERSES

KEY POINTS

APPLICATION

# Prayer journal

DATE _____

TODAY'S PASSAGE          PREACHER          SERMON TOPIC

NOTES

KEY VERSES

PRAYER

KEY POINTS

APPLICATION

# Prayer journal

DATE _____

TODAY'S PASSAGE          PREACHER          SERMON TOPIC

NOTES
_____
_____
_____
_____
_____
_____
_____
_____
_____
_____
_____
_____

| KEY VERSES |
| --- |
| |

PRAYER
_____
_____
_____
_____
_____
_____
_____

| KEY POINTS |
| --- |
| |

_____
_____
_____
_____
_____
_____
_____
_____
_____

| APPLICATION |
| --- |
| |

# Prayer journal

DATE _____

TODAY'S PASSAGE          PREACHER          SERMON TOPIC

NOTES
_____
_____
_____
_____
_____
_____
_____
_____
_____
_____
_____
_____

PRAYER
_____
_____
_____
_____
_____
_____
_____
_____
_____
_____
_____
_____
_____
_____
_____

KEY VERSES

KEY POINTS

APPLICATION

# Prayer journal

DATE _____

TODAY'S PASSAGE          PREACHER                    SERMON TOPIC

NOTES
_____
_____
_____
_____
_____
_____
_____
_____
_____
_____
_____

KEY VERSES

PRAYER
_____
_____
_____
_____
_____
_____
_____

KEY POINTS

_____
_____
_____
_____
_____
_____
_____
_____

APPLICATION

# Prayer journal

DATE _____

TODAY'S PASSAGE          PREACHER          SERMON TOPIC

NOTES
_____
_____
_____
_____
_____
_____
_____
_____
_____
_____
_____

| KEY VERSES |
| --- |
|  |

PRAYER
_____
_____
_____
_____
_____
_____
_____

| KEY POINTS |
| --- |
|  |

_____
_____
_____
_____
_____
_____
_____
_____
_____
_____

| APPLICATION |
| --- |
|  |

# Prayer journal

DATE

TODAY'S PASSAGE          PREACHER          SERMON TOPIC

NOTES

| KEY VERSES |
| --- |

PRAYER

| KEY POINTS |
| --- |

| APPLICATION |
| --- |

# Prayer journal

DATE _____

TODAY'S PASSAGE          PREACHER          SERMON TOPIC

NOTES
_____
_____
_____
_____
_____
_____
_____
_____
_____
_____
_____

PRAYER
_____
_____
_____
_____
_____
_____
_____
_____
_____
_____
_____
_____
_____
_____
_____

KEY VERSES

KEY POINTS

APPLICATION

# Prayer journal

DATE _____

TODAY'S PASSAGE          PREACHER          SERMON TOPIC

NOTES
_____
_____
_____
_____
_____
_____
_____
_____
_____
_____
_____
_____
_____

PRAYER
_____
_____
_____
_____
_____
_____
_____
_____
_____
_____
_____
_____
_____
_____
_____
_____
_____

KEY VERSES

KEY POINTS

APPLICATION

# Prayer journal

DATE _____

TODAY'S PASSAGE          PREACHER          SERMON TOPIC

NOTES
_____
_____
_____
_____
_____
_____
_____
_____
_____
_____
_____

PRAYER
_____
_____
_____
_____
_____
_____
_____
_____
_____
_____
_____
_____
_____
_____
_____
_____

| KEY VERSES |
| --- |
|  |

| KEY POINTS |
| --- |
|  |

| APPLICATION |
| --- |
|  |

# Prayer journal

DATE _____

TODAY'S PASSAGE          PREACHER          SERMON TOPIC

NOTES
_____
_____
_____
_____
_____
_____
_____
_____
_____
_____
_____
_____

PRAYER
_____
_____
_____
_____
_____
_____
_____
_____
_____
_____
_____
_____
_____
_____
_____
_____
_____

KEY VERSES

KEY POINTS

APPLICATION

# Prayer journal

DATE _____

TODAY'S PASSAGE          PREACHER          SERMON TOPIC

NOTES
_____
_____
_____
_____
_____
_____
_____
_____
_____
_____
_____
_____
_____

PRAYER
_____
_____
_____
_____
_____
_____
_____
_____
_____
_____
_____
_____
_____
_____
_____
_____

KEY VERSES

KEY POINTS

APPLICATION

# Prayer journal

DATE _____

TODAY'S PASSAGE          PREACHER                    SERMON TOPIC

NOTES
_____
_____
_____
_____
_____
_____
_____
_____
_____
_____
_____
_____

PRAYER
_____
_____
_____
_____
_____
_____
_____
_____
_____
_____
_____
_____
_____
_____
_____
_____

KEY VERSES

KEY POINTS

APPLICATION

# Prayer journal

DATE _____

TODAY'S PASSAGE          PREACHER          SERMON TOPIC

NOTES
_____
_____
_____
_____
_____
_____
_____
_____
_____
_____
_____

| KEY VERSES |
| --- |
|  |

PRAYER
_____
_____
_____
_____
_____
_____
_____

| KEY POINTS |
| --- |
|  |

_____
_____
_____
_____
_____
_____
_____
_____
_____
_____

| APPLICATION |
| --- |
|  |

# Prayer journal

DATE

TODAY'S PASSAGE          PREACHER          SERMON TOPIC

NOTES

KEY VERSES

PRAYER

KEY POINTS

APPLICATION

# Prayer journal

DATE _____

TODAY'S PASSAGE      PREACHER      SERMON TOPIC

NOTES

_____

_____

_____

_____

_____

_____

_____

_____

_____

_____

_____

_____

PRAYER

_____

_____

_____

_____

_____

_____

_____

_____

_____

_____

_____

_____

_____

_____

KEY VERSES

KEY POINTS

APPLICATION

# Prayer journal

DATE

TODAY'S PASSAGE          PREACHER          SERMON TOPIC

NOTES

_____
_____
_____
_____
_____
_____
_____
_____
_____
_____
_____
_____

PRAYER

_____
_____
_____
_____
_____
_____
_____
_____
_____
_____
_____
_____
_____
_____
_____
_____
_____

| KEY VERSES |
| --- |
|  |

| KEY POINTS |
| --- |
|  |

| APPLICATION |
| --- |
|  |

DATE

# Prayer journal

TODAY'S PASSAGE          PREACHER          SERMON TOPIC

NOTES

_____

_____

_____

_____

_____

_____

_____

_____

_____

_____

_____

PRAYER

_____

_____

_____

_____

_____

_____

_____

_____

_____

_____

_____

_____

_____

_____

KEY VERSES

KEY POINTS

APPLICATION

# Prayer journal

DATE _____

TODAY'S PASSAGE          PREACHER          SERMON TOPIC

NOTES
_____
_____
_____
_____
_____
_____
_____
_____
_____
_____
_____

PRAYER
_____
_____
_____
_____
_____
_____
_____
_____
_____
_____
_____
_____
_____
_____
_____
_____

KEY VERSES

KEY POINTS

APPLICATION

# Prayer journal

DATE _____

TODAY'S PASSAGE          PREACHER          SERMON TOPIC

NOTES
_____
_____
_____
_____
_____
_____
_____
_____
_____
_____
_____

KEY VERSES

PRAYER
_____
_____
_____
_____
_____
_____
_____
_____
_____
_____
_____
_____
_____
_____
_____

KEY POINTS

APPLICATION

# Prayer journal

DATE _____

TODAY'S PASSAGE      PREACHER      SERMON TOPIC

NOTES
_____
_____
_____
_____
_____
_____
_____
_____
_____
_____
_____

PRAYER
_____
_____
_____
_____
_____
_____
_____
_____
_____
_____
_____
_____
_____
_____
_____
_____
_____

KEY VERSES

KEY POINTS

APPLICATION

# Prayer journal

DATE _____

TODAY'S PASSAGE          PREACHER                    SERMON TOPIC

NOTES
_____
_____
_____
_____
_____
_____
_____
_____
_____
_____
_____

| KEY VERSES |
| --- |
|  |

PRAYER
_____
_____
_____
_____
_____
_____
_____

| KEY POINTS |
| --- |
|  |

_____
_____
_____
_____
_____
_____
_____
_____
_____

| APPLICATION |
| --- |
|  |

# Prayer journal

DATE _____

TODAY'S PASSAGE          PREACHER          SERMON TOPIC

NOTES
_____
_____
_____
_____
_____
_____
_____
_____
_____
_____
_____
_____

PRAYER
_____
_____
_____
_____
_____
_____
_____
_____
_____
_____
_____
_____
_____
_____
_____
_____
_____

KEY VERSES

KEY POINTS

APPLICATION

# Prayer journal

DATE _____

TODAY'S PASSAGE          PREACHER          SERMON TOPIC

NOTES
_____
_____
_____
_____
_____
_____
_____
_____
_____
_____
_____
_____

| KEY VERSES |
| --- |
|  |

PRAYER
_____
_____
_____
_____
_____
_____
_____
_____
_____
_____
_____
_____
_____
_____
_____
_____

| KEY POINTS |
| --- |
|  |

| APPLICATION |
| --- |
|  |

# Prayer journal

DATE

TODAY'S PASSAGE          PREACHER          SERMON TOPIC

NOTES

KEY VERSES

PRAYER

KEY POINTS

APPLICATION

# Prayer journal

DATE _____

TODAY'S PASSAGE          PREACHER          SERMON TOPIC

NOTES
_____
_____
_____
_____
_____
_____
_____
_____
_____
_____
_____
_____

PRAYER
_____
_____
_____
_____
_____
_____
_____
_____
_____
_____
_____
_____
_____
_____
_____
_____

KEY VERSES

KEY POINTS

APPLICATION

# Prayer journal

DATE

TODAY'S PASSAGE          PREACHER          SERMON TOPIC

NOTES

_____
_____
_____
_____
_____
_____
_____
_____
_____
_____

| KEY VERSES |
| --- |
| |

PRAYER

_____
_____
_____
_____
_____
_____
_____
_____
_____
_____
_____
_____
_____
_____
_____
_____
_____

| KEY POINTS |
| --- |
| |

| APPLICATION |
| --- |
| |

# Prayer journal

DATE _____

TODAY'S PASSAGE          PREACHER                SERMON TOPIC

NOTES
_____
_____
_____
_____
_____
_____
_____
_____
_____
_____
_____

KEY VERSES

PRAYER
_____
_____
_____
_____
_____
_____
_____
_____
_____
_____
_____
_____
_____
_____
_____

KEY POINTS

APPLICATION

# Prayer journal

DATE _____

TODAY'S PASSAGE          PREACHER          SERMON TOPIC

NOTES
_____
_____
_____
_____
_____
_____
_____
_____
_____
_____
_____
_____

PRAYER
_____
_____
_____
_____
_____
_____
_____
_____
_____
_____
_____
_____
_____
_____
_____
_____

| KEY VERSES |
| --- |
|  |

| KEY POINTS |
| --- |
|  |

| APPLICATION |
| --- |
|  |

# Prayer journal

DATE

TODAY'S PASSAGE          PREACHER          SERMON TOPIC

NOTES

KEY VERSES

PRAYER

KEY POINTS

APPLICATION

# Prayer journal

DATE _____

TODAY'S PASSAGE      PREACHER      SERMON TOPIC

NOTES
_____
_____
_____
_____
_____
_____
_____
_____
_____
_____
_____

PRAYER
_____
_____
_____
_____
_____
_____
_____
_____
_____
_____
_____
_____
_____

KEY VERSES

KEY POINTS

APPLICATION

# Prayer journal

DATE _____

TODAY'S PASSAGE          PREACHER                    SERMON TOPIC

NOTES
_____
_____
_____
_____
_____
_____
_____
_____
_____
_____
_____
_____
_____

PRAYER
_____
_____
_____
_____
_____
_____
_____
_____
_____
_____
_____
_____
_____
_____
_____
_____

KEY VERSES

KEY POINTS

APPLICATION

# Prayer journal

DATE _____

TODAY'S PASSAGE      PREACHER      SERMON TOPIC

NOTES
_____
_____
_____
_____
_____
_____
_____
_____
_____
_____
_____
_____
_____

PRAYER
_____
_____
_____
_____
_____
_____
_____
_____
_____
_____
_____
_____
_____
_____
_____

KEY VERSES

KEY POINTS

APPLICATION

# Prayer journal

DATE _____

TODAY'S PASSAGE                PREACHER                SERMON TOPIC

NOTES
_____
_____
_____
_____
_____
_____
_____
_____
_____
_____
_____
_____
_____

PRAYER
_____
_____
_____
_____
_____
_____
_____
_____
_____
_____
_____
_____
_____
_____
_____
_____

| KEY VERSES |
| --- |
|  |

| KEY POINTS |
| --- |
|  |

| APPLICATION |
| --- |
|  |

# Prayer journal

DATE _____

TODAY'S PASSAGE          PREACHER          SERMON TOPIC

NOTES
_____
_____
_____
_____
_____
_____
_____
_____
_____
_____
_____
_____

PRAYER
_____
_____
_____
_____
_____
_____
_____
_____
_____
_____
_____
_____
_____
_____
_____
_____

| KEY VERSES |
| --- |
| |

| KEY POINTS |
| --- |
| |

| APPLICATION |
| --- |
| |

# Prayer journal

DATE _____

TODAY'S PASSAGE          PREACHER          SERMON TOPIC

NOTES

_____

_____

_____

_____

_____

_____

_____

_____

_____

_____

_____

_____

PRAYER

_____

_____

_____

_____

_____

_____

_____

_____

_____

_____

_____

_____

_____

_____

_____

| KEY VERSES |
| --- |
| |

| KEY POINTS |
| --- |
| |

| APPLICATION |
| --- |
| |

# Prayer journal

DATE _____

TODAY'S PASSAGE          PREACHER          SERMON TOPIC

NOTES
_____
_____
_____
_____
_____
_____
_____
_____
_____
_____
_____
_____

PRAYER
_____
_____
_____
_____
_____
_____
_____
_____
_____
_____
_____
_____
_____
_____
_____
_____

KEY VERSES

KEY POINTS

APPLICATION

# Prayer journal

DATE _____

TODAY'S PASSAGE          PREACHER          SERMON TOPIC

NOTES
_____
_____
_____
_____
_____
_____
_____
_____
_____
_____
_____
_____

PRAYER
_____
_____
_____
_____
_____
_____
_____
_____
_____
_____
_____
_____
_____
_____
_____

KEY VERSES

KEY POINTS

APPLICATION

# Prayer journal

DATE _____

TODAY'S PASSAGE          PREACHER          SERMON TOPIC

NOTES
_____
_____
_____
_____
_____
_____
_____
_____
_____
_____
_____

| KEY VERSES |
| --- |
|  |

PRAYER
_____
_____
_____
_____
_____
_____
_____

| KEY POINTS |
| --- |
|  |

_____
_____
_____
_____
_____
_____
_____
_____

| APPLICATION |
| --- |
|  |

# Prayer journal

DATE _____

TODAY'S PASSAGE          PREACHER          SERMON TOPIC

NOTES
_____
_____
_____
_____
_____
_____
_____
_____
_____
_____
_____
_____

PRAYER
_____
_____
_____
_____
_____
_____
_____
_____
_____
_____
_____
_____
_____
_____

KEY VERSES

KEY POINTS

APPLICATION

# Prayer journal

DATE

TODAY'S PASSAGE          PREACHER          SERMON TOPIC

NOTES

KEY VERSES

KEY POINTS

PRAYER

APPLICATION

# Prayer journal

DATE _____

TODAY'S PASSAGE     PREACHER     SERMON TOPIC

NOTES

KEY VERSES

PRAYER

KEY POINTS

APPLICATION

# Prayer journal

DATE _____

TODAY'S PASSAGE       PREACHER       SERMON TOPIC

NOTES
_____
_____
_____
_____
_____
_____
_____
_____
_____
_____
_____

| KEY VERSES |
|---|
| |

PRAYER
_____
_____
_____
_____
_____
_____
_____
_____

| KEY POINTS |
|---|
| |

_____
_____
_____
_____
_____
_____
_____
_____

| APPLICATION |
|---|
| |

# Prayer journal

DATE _____

TODAY'S PASSAGE       PREACHER       SERMON TOPIC

NOTES
_____
_____
_____
_____
_____
_____
_____
_____
_____
_____
_____
_____

PRAYER
_____
_____
_____
_____
_____
_____
_____
_____
_____
_____
_____
_____
_____
_____
_____

KEY VERSES

KEY POINTS

APPLICATION

# Prayer journal

DATE _____

TODAY'S PASSAGE          PREACHER          SERMON TOPIC

NOTES
_____
_____
_____
_____
_____
_____
_____
_____
_____
_____
_____

PRAYER
_____
_____
_____
_____
_____
_____
_____
_____
_____
_____
_____
_____
_____
_____

KEY VERSES

KEY POINTS

APPLICATION

# Prayer journal

DATE _____

TODAY'S PASSAGE _____  PREACHER _____  SERMON TOPIC _____

NOTES
_____
_____
_____
_____
_____
_____
_____
_____
_____
_____
_____

PRAYER
_____
_____
_____
_____
_____
_____
_____
_____
_____
_____
_____
_____
_____
_____

| KEY VERSES |
|---|
|  |

| KEY POINTS |
|---|
|  |

| APPLICATION |
|---|
|  |

# Prayer journal

DATE _____

TODAY'S PASSAGE          PREACHER                    SERMON TOPIC

NOTES
_____
_____
_____
_____
_____
_____
_____
_____
_____
_____
_____

KEY VERSES

PRAYER
_____
_____
_____
_____
_____
_____
_____
_____
_____
_____
_____
_____
_____
_____

KEY POINTS

APPLICATION

# Prayer journal

DATE _____

TODAY'S PASSAGE          PREACHER          SERMON TOPIC

NOTES
_____

KEY VERSES

PRAYER
_____

KEY POINTS

APPLICATION

# Prayer journal

DATE

TODAY'S PASSAGE          PREACHER          SERMON TOPIC

NOTES

KEY VERSES

PRAYER

KEY POINTS

APPLICATION

# Prayer journal

DATE _____

TODAY'S PASSAGE          PREACHER          SERMON TOPIC

NOTES
_____
_____
_____
_____
_____
_____
_____
_____
_____
_____

| KEY VERSES |
| --- |
| |

PRAYER
_____
_____
_____
_____
_____
_____

| KEY POINTS |
| --- |
| |

_____
_____
_____
_____
_____
_____
_____
_____
_____
_____

| APPLICATION |
| --- |
| |

# Prayer journal

DATE _____

TODAY'S PASSAGE                    PREACHER                    SERMON TOPIC

NOTES

---

---

---

---

---

---

---

---

---

---

---

KEY VERSES

PRAYER

---

---

---

---

---

---

---

KEY POINTS

---

---

---

---

---

---

---

---

---

---

---

APPLICATION

DATE _____

# Prayer journal

TODAY'S PASSAGE          PREACHER                    SERMON TOPIC

NOTES
_____

| KEY VERSES |
| --- |
|  |

PRAYER
_____

| KEY POINTS |
| --- |
|  |

| APPLICATION |
| --- |
|  |

# Prayer journal

DATE _____

TODAY'S PASSAGE _____  PREACHER _____  SERMON TOPIC _____

NOTES
_____
_____
_____
_____
_____
_____
_____
_____
_____
_____
_____

PRAYER
_____
_____
_____
_____
_____
_____
_____
_____
_____
_____
_____
_____
_____
_____
_____
_____
_____

KEY VERSES

KEY POINTS

APPLICATION

# Prayer journal

DATE _____

TODAY'S PASSAGE                    PREACHER                    SERMON TOPIC

NOTES
_____
_____
_____
_____
_____
_____
_____
_____
_____
_____

| KEY VERSES |
| :-: |
| |

PRAYER
_____
_____
_____
_____
_____
_____
_____

| KEY POINTS |
| :-: |
| |

_____
_____
_____
_____
_____
_____
_____
_____
_____

| APPLICATION |
| :-: |
| |

# Prayer journal

DATE _____

TODAY'S PASSAGE      PREACHER      SERMON TOPIC

NOTES
_____
_____
_____
_____
_____
_____
_____
_____
_____
_____
_____

PRAYER
_____
_____
_____
_____
_____
_____
_____
_____
_____
_____
_____
_____
_____
_____

## KEY VERSES

## KEY POINTS

## APPLICATION

# Prayer journal

DATE _____

TODAY'S PASSAGE          PREACHER                    SERMON TOPIC

NOTES
_____
_____
_____
_____
_____
_____
_____
_____
_____
_____
_____

KEY VERSES

PRAYER
_____
_____
_____
_____
_____
_____
_____
_____

KEY POINTS

_____
_____
_____
_____
_____
_____
_____
_____

APPLICATION

DATE _____

# Prayer journal

TODAY'S PASSAGE          PREACHER          SERMON TOPIC

NOTES
_____
_____
_____
_____
_____
_____
_____
_____
_____

| KEY VERSES |
| --- |
|  |

PRAYER
_____
_____
_____
_____
_____
_____

| KEY POINTS |
| --- |
|  |

_____
_____
_____
_____
_____
_____
_____
_____

| APPLICATION |
| --- |
|  |

# Prayer journal

DATE _____

TODAY'S PASSAGE          PREACHER          SERMON TOPIC

NOTES
_____
_____
_____
_____
_____
_____
_____
_____
_____
_____
_____

PRAYER
_____
_____
_____
_____
_____
_____
_____
_____
_____
_____
_____
_____
_____
_____

KEY VERSES

KEY POINTS

APPLICATION

DATE _____

# Prayer journal

TODAY'S PASSAGE          PREACHER          SERMON TOPIC

NOTES
_____
_____
_____
_____
_____
_____
_____
_____
_____

_____
_____

| KEY VERSES |
| --- |
|  |

PRAYER
_____
_____
_____
_____
_____
_____
_____

| KEY POINTS |
| --- |
|  |

_____
_____
_____
_____
_____
_____
_____
_____
_____

| APPLICATION |
| --- |
|  |

# Prayer journal

DATE _____

TODAY'S PASSAGE          PREACHER          SERMON TOPIC

NOTES
_____
_____
_____
_____
_____
_____
_____
_____
_____

| KEY VERSES |
| --- |
|  |

PRAYER
_____
_____
_____
_____
_____
_____

| KEY POINTS |
| --- |
|  |

_____
_____
_____
_____
_____
_____
_____
_____
_____

| APPLICATION |
| --- |
|  |

DATE _____

# Prayer journal

TODAY'S PASSAGE      PREACHER      SERMON TOPIC

NOTES
_____
_____
_____
_____
_____
_____
_____
_____
_____
_____
_____

PRAYER
_____
_____
_____
_____
_____
_____
_____
_____
_____
_____
_____
_____
_____
_____
_____
_____
_____

KEY VERSES

KEY POINTS

APPLICATION

DATE _____

# Prayer journal

TODAY'S PASSAGE          PREACHER          SERMON TOPIC

NOTES
_____

_____

_____

_____

_____

_____

_____

_____

_____

_____

_____

PRAYER
_____

_____

_____

_____

_____

_____

_____

_____

_____

_____

_____

_____

_____

_____

| KEY VERSES |
| --- |
| |

| KEY POINTS |
| --- |
| |

| APPLICATION |
| --- |
| |

# Prayer journal

DATE _____

TODAY'S PASSAGE        PREACHER        SERMON TOPIC

NOTES
_____
_____
_____
_____
_____
_____
_____
_____
_____
_____
_____

| KEY VERSES |
| --- |
|  |

PRAYER
_____
_____
_____
_____
_____
_____

| KEY POINTS |
| --- |
|  |

_____
_____
_____
_____
_____
_____
_____
_____
_____

| APPLICATION |
| --- |
|  |

DATE _____

# Prayer journal

TODAY'S PASSAGE                    PREACHER                    SERMON TOPIC

NOTES
_____
_____
_____
_____
_____
_____
_____
_____
_____
_____
_____

| KEY VERSES |
| :---: |
|  |

PRAYER
_____
_____
_____
_____
_____
_____
_____

| KEY POINTS |
| :---: |
|  |

_____
_____
_____
_____
_____
_____
_____
_____

| APPLICATION |
| :---: |
|  |

# Prayer journal

DATE _____

TODAY'S PASSAGE          PREACHER          SERMON TOPIC

NOTES
_____
_____
_____
_____
_____
_____
_____
_____
_____
_____
_____

KEY VERSES

PRAYER
_____
_____
_____
_____
_____
_____

KEY POINTS

_____
_____
_____
_____
_____
_____
_____

APPLICATION

# Prayer journal

DATE _____

TODAY'S PASSAGE      PREACHER      SERMON TOPIC

NOTES

_____

_____

_____

_____

_____

_____

_____

_____

_____

_____

_____

PRAYER

_____

_____

_____

_____

_____

_____

_____

_____

_____

_____

_____

_____

_____

KEY VERSES

KEY POINTS

APPLICATION

# Prayer journal

DATE _____

TODAY'S PASSAGE _____    PREACHER _____    SERMON TOPIC _____

NOTES
_____
_____
_____
_____
_____
_____
_____
_____
_____
_____

| KEY VERSES |
| --- |
| |

PRAYER
_____
_____
_____
_____
_____
_____
_____

| KEY POINTS |
| --- |
| |

_____
_____
_____
_____
_____
_____
_____
_____

| APPLICATION |
| --- |
| |

# Prayer journal

DATE _____

TODAY'S PASSAGE _____ PREACHER _____ SERMON TOPIC _____

NOTES
_____
_____
_____
_____
_____
_____
_____
_____
_____
_____
_____
_____
_____

PRAYER
_____
_____
_____
_____
_____
_____
_____
_____
_____
_____
_____
_____
_____
_____
_____
_____

| KEY VERSES |
| --- |
| |

| KEY POINTS |
| --- |
| |

| APPLICATION |
| --- |
| |

DATE

# *Prayer journal*

TODAY'S PASSAGE

PREACHER

SERMON TOPIC

NOTES

KEY VERSES

PRAYER

KEY POINTS

APPLICATION

# Prayer journal

DATE _____

TODAY'S PASSAGE          PREACHER          SERMON TOPIC

NOTES
_____
_____
_____
_____
_____
_____
_____
_____
_____
_____
_____

PRAYER
_____
_____
_____
_____
_____
_____
_____
_____
_____
_____
_____
_____
_____
_____
_____

KEY VERSES

KEY POINTS

APPLICATION

# Prayer journal

DATE _____

TODAY'S PASSAGE     PREACHER     SERMON TOPIC

NOTES
_____
_____
_____
_____
_____
_____
_____
_____
_____
_____
_____
_____

PRAYER
_____
_____
_____
_____
_____
_____
_____
_____
_____
_____
_____
_____
_____
_____
_____

KEY VERSES

KEY POINTS

APPLICATION

DATE _____

# Prayer journal

TODAY'S PASSAGE          PREACHER          SERMON TOPIC

NOTES
_____

| KEY VERSES |
|---|
|  |

PRAYER
_____

| KEY POINTS |
|---|
|  |

| APPLICATION |
|---|
|  |

# Prayer journal

DATE _____

TODAY'S PASSAGE _____  PREACHER _____  SERMON TOPIC _____

NOTES
_____
_____
_____
_____
_____
_____
_____
_____
_____
_____

| KEY VERSES |
| --- |
| |

_____
_____

| KEY POINTS |
| --- |
| |

PRAYER
_____
_____
_____
_____
_____
_____
_____

| APPLICATION |
| --- |
| |

_____
_____
_____
_____
_____
_____
_____
_____
_____
_____

DATE _____

# Prayer journal

TODAY'S PASSAGE          PREACHER                    SERMON TOPIC

NOTES
_____
_____
_____
_____
_____
_____
_____
_____
_____
_____
_____
_____
_____

PRAYER
_____
_____
_____
_____
_____
_____
_____
_____
_____
_____
_____
_____
_____
_____
_____
_____

| KEY VERSES |
| --- |
| |

| KEY POINTS |
| --- |
| |

| APPLICATION |
| --- |
| |

# Prayer journal

DATE _____

TODAY'S PASSAGE        PREACHER        SERMON TOPIC

NOTES
_____
_____
_____
_____
_____
_____
_____
_____
_____
_____
_____
_____

PRAYER
_____
_____
_____
_____
_____
_____
_____
_____
_____
_____
_____
_____
_____
_____
_____
_____

KEY VERSES

KEY POINTS

APPLICATION

# Prayer journal

DATE _____

TODAY'S PASSAGE          PREACHER          SERMON TOPIC

NOTES
_____
_____
_____
_____
_____
_____
_____
_____
_____
_____
_____

| KEY VERSES |
| --- |
|  |

PRAYER
_____
_____
_____
_____
_____
_____

| KEY POINTS |
| --- |
|  |

_____
_____
_____
_____
_____
_____
_____
_____
_____

| APPLICATION |
| --- |
|  |

DATE _____

# Prayer journal

TODAY'S PASSAGE          PREACHER          SERMON TOPIC

NOTES
_____
_____
_____
_____
_____
_____
_____
_____
_____
_____
_____

KEY VERSES

PRAYER
_____
_____
_____
_____
_____
_____
_____
_____
_____
_____
_____
_____
_____
_____
_____

KEY POINTS

APPLICATION

# Prayer journal

DATE _____

TODAY'S PASSAGE                PREACHER                SERMON TOPIC

NOTES
_____
_____
_____
_____
_____
_____
_____
_____
_____
_____
_____
_____

PRAYER
_____
_____
_____
_____
_____
_____
_____
_____
_____
_____
_____
_____
_____
_____
_____

KEY VERSES

KEY POINTS

APPLICATION

# Prayer journal

DATE _____

TODAY'S PASSAGE          PREACHER          SERMON TOPIC

NOTES
_____
_____
_____
_____
_____
_____
_____
_____
_____
_____
_____
_____

PRAYER
_____
_____
_____
_____
_____
_____
_____
_____
_____
_____
_____
_____
_____
_____
_____
_____

KEY VERSES

KEY POINTS

APPLICATION

# Prayer journal

DATE _____

TODAY'S PASSAGE          PREACHER          SERMON TOPIC

NOTES
_____
_____
_____
_____
_____
_____
_____
_____
_____
_____
_____
_____
_____

| KEY VERSES |
| --- |
|  |

PRAYER
_____
_____
_____
_____
_____
_____
_____

| KEY POINTS |
| --- |
|  |

_____
_____
_____
_____
_____
_____
_____
_____
_____
_____
_____

| APPLICATION |
| --- |
|  |

# Prayer journal

DATE _____

TODAY'S PASSAGE          PREACHER          SERMON TOPIC

NOTES
_____
_____
_____
_____
_____
_____
_____
_____
_____
_____

PRAYER
_____
_____
_____
_____
_____
_____
_____
_____
_____
_____
_____
_____
_____
_____

KEY VERSES

KEY POINTS

APPLICATION

# Prayer journal

DATE _____

TODAY'S PASSAGE          PREACHER                    SERMON TOPIC

NOTES
_____
_____
_____
_____
_____
_____
_____
_____
_____
_____
_____

PRAYER
_____
_____
_____
_____
_____
_____
_____
_____
_____
_____
_____
_____
_____
_____
_____

KEY VERSES

KEY POINTS

APPLICATION

# Prayer journal

DATE _____

TODAY'S PASSAGE          PREACHER          SERMON TOPIC

NOTES
_____
_____
_____
_____
_____
_____
_____
_____
_____
_____
_____

KEY VERSES

PRAYER
_____
_____
_____
_____
_____
_____
_____
_____
_____
_____
_____
_____
_____
_____
_____
_____

KEY POINTS

APPLICATION

# Prayer journal

DATE _____

TODAY'S PASSAGE          PREACHER          SERMON TOPIC

NOTES

_____
_____
_____
_____
_____
_____
_____
_____
_____
_____
_____
_____

PRAYER

_____
_____
_____
_____
_____
_____
_____
_____
_____
_____
_____
_____
_____
_____
_____
_____

KEY VERSES

KEY POINTS

APPLICATION

DATE _____

# Prayer journal

TODAY'S PASSAGE      PREACHER      SERMON TOPIC

NOTES

_____
_____
_____
_____
_____
_____
_____
_____
_____
_____
_____

| KEY VERSES |
| --- |
| |

PRAYER

_____
_____
_____
_____
_____
_____
_____
_____
_____
_____
_____
_____
_____
_____
_____
_____
_____

| KEY POINTS |
| --- |
| |

| APPLICATION |
| --- |
| |

# Prayer journal

DATE _____

TODAY'S PASSAGE                    PREACHER                    SERMON TOPIC

NOTES
_____
_____
_____
_____
_____
_____
_____
_____
_____
_____
_____
_____

| KEY VERSES |
| --- |
|  |

PRAYER
_____
_____
_____
_____
_____
_____
_____
_____
_____
_____
_____
_____
_____
_____
_____
_____

| KEY POINTS |
| --- |
|  |

| APPLICATION |
| --- |
|  |

# Prayer journal

DATE _____

TODAY'S PASSAGE          PREACHER          SERMON TOPIC

NOTES

KEY VERSES

PRAYER

KEY POINTS

APPLICATION

# Prayer journal

DATE _____

TODAY'S PASSAGE          PREACHER                    SERMON TOPIC

NOTES
_____
_____
_____
_____
_____
_____
_____
_____
_____
_____
_____

PRAYER
_____
_____
_____
_____
_____
_____
_____
_____
_____
_____
_____
_____
_____
_____
_____

KEY VERSES

KEY POINTS

APPLICATION

# Prayer journal

DATE _____

TODAY'S PASSAGE                PREACHER                SERMON TOPIC

NOTES
_____
_____
_____
_____
_____
_____
_____
_____
_____
_____
_____
_____

PRAYER
_____
_____
_____
_____
_____
_____
_____
_____
_____
_____
_____
_____
_____
_____
_____
_____
_____

KEY VERSES

KEY POINTS

APPLICATION

DATE _____

# Prayer journal

TODAY'S PASSAGE          PREACHER          SERMON TOPIC

NOTES
_____

| KEY VERSES |
|:----------:|
|            |

PRAYER
_____

| KEY POINTS |
|:----------:|
|            |

| APPLICATION |
|:-----------:|
|             |

# Prayer journal

DATE

TODAY'S PASSAGE

PREACHER

SERMON TOPIC

NOTES

PRAYER

KEY VERSES

KEY POINTS

APPLICATION

# Prayer journal

DATE _____

TODAY'S PASSAGE          PREACHER          SERMON TOPIC

NOTES
_____
_____
_____
_____
_____
_____
_____
_____
_____
_____
_____

| KEY VERSES |
| --- |
| |

PRAYER
_____
_____
_____
_____
_____
_____
_____

| KEY POINTS |
| --- |
| |

_____
_____
_____
_____
_____
_____
_____
_____
_____

| APPLICATION |
| --- |
| |

DATE

# *Prayer journal*

TODAY'S PASSAGE          PREACHER          SERMON TOPIC

NOTES

KEY VERSES

PRAYER

KEY POINTS

APPLICATION

# Prayer journal

DATE _____

TODAY'S PASSAGE          PREACHER          SERMON TOPIC

NOTES
_____
_____
_____
_____
_____
_____
_____
_____
_____
_____
_____

PRAYER
_____
_____
_____
_____
_____
_____
_____
_____
_____
_____
_____
_____
_____
_____
_____
_____

KEY VERSES

KEY POINTS

APPLICATION

DATE _____

# Prayer journal

TODAY'S PASSAGE      PREACHER      SERMON TOPIC

NOTES
_____
_____
_____
_____
_____
_____
_____
_____
_____
_____
_____

PRAYER
_____
_____
_____
_____
_____
_____
_____
_____
_____
_____
_____
_____
_____
_____
_____
_____
_____

| KEY VERSES |
| --- |
|  |

| KEY POINTS |
| --- |
|  |

| APPLICATION |
| --- |
|  |

# Prayer journal

DATE _____

TODAY'S PASSAGE                 PREACHER                 SERMON TOPIC

NOTES
_____
_____
_____
_____
_____
_____
_____
_____
_____
_____
_____
_____

| KEY VERSES |
| --- |
| |

PRAYER
_____
_____
_____
_____
_____
_____
_____

| KEY POINTS |
| --- |
| |

_____
_____
_____
_____
_____
_____
_____
_____

| APPLICATION |
| --- |
| |

# Prayer journal

DATE _____

TODAY'S PASSAGE          PREACHER          SERMON TOPIC

NOTES
_____
_____
_____
_____
_____
_____
_____
_____
_____
_____
_____

PRAYER
_____
_____
_____
_____
_____
_____
_____
_____
_____
_____
_____
_____
_____
_____
_____
_____

KEY VERSES

KEY POINTS

APPLICATION

# Prayer journal

DATE _____

TODAY'S PASSAGE          PREACHER          SERMON TOPIC

NOTES
_____
_____
_____
_____
_____
_____
_____
_____
_____
_____
_____

PRAYER
_____
_____
_____
_____
_____
_____
_____
_____
_____
_____
_____
_____
_____

KEY VERSES

KEY POINTS

APPLICATION

# Prayer journal

DATE _____

TODAY'S PASSAGE          PREACHER          SERMON TOPIC

NOTES
_____
_____
_____
_____
_____
_____
_____
_____
_____
_____
_____

KEY VERSES

PRAYER
_____
_____
_____
_____
_____
_____
_____
_____
_____
_____
_____
_____
_____
_____
_____
_____

KEY POINTS

APPLICATION

DATE _____

# Prayer journal

TODAY'S PASSAGE          PREACHER          SERMON TOPIC

NOTES
_____
_____
_____
_____
_____
_____
_____
_____
_____
_____
_____

| KEY VERSES |
| --- |
| |

PRAYER
_____
_____
_____
_____
_____
_____
_____

| KEY POINTS |
| --- |
| |

_____
_____
_____
_____
_____
_____
_____
_____

| APPLICATION |
| --- |
| |

# Prayer journal

DATE _____

TODAY'S PASSAGE          PREACHER          SERMON TOPIC

NOTES
_____
_____
_____
_____
_____
_____
_____
_____
_____
_____

| KEY VERSES |
| --- |
| |

PRAYER
_____
_____
_____
_____
_____
_____
_____

| KEY POINTS |
| --- |
| |

_____
_____
_____
_____
_____
_____
_____
_____
_____
_____

| APPLICATION |
| --- |
| |

# Prayer journal

DATE _____

TODAY'S PASSAGE          PREACHER          SERMON TOPIC

NOTES
_____
_____
_____
_____
_____
_____
_____
_____
_____
_____
_____

KEY VERSES

PRAYER
_____
_____
_____
_____
_____
_____
_____
_____
_____
_____
_____
_____
_____
_____
_____
_____

KEY POINTS

APPLICATION

DATE _____

# Prayer journal

TODAY'S PASSAGE          PREACHER          SERMON TOPIC

NOTES
_____
_____
_____
_____
_____
_____
_____
_____
_____
_____
_____
_____

| KEY VERSES |
| --- |
|  |
|  |
|  |
|  |
|  |
|  |

PRAYER
_____
_____
_____
_____
_____
_____
_____
_____
_____
_____
_____
_____
_____
_____
_____
_____

| KEY POINTS |
| --- |
|  |
|  |
|  |
|  |

| APPLICATION |
| --- |
|  |
|  |
|  |
|  |

# Prayer journal

DATE _____

TODAY'S PASSAGE          PREACHER          SERMON TOPIC

NOTES
_____
_____
_____
_____
_____
_____
_____
_____
_____
_____
_____

PRAYER
_____
_____
_____
_____
_____
_____
_____
_____
_____
_____
_____
_____
_____
_____

KEY VERSES

KEY POINTS

APPLICATION

# Prayer journal

DATE _____

TODAY'S PASSAGE      PREACHER      SERMON TOPIC

NOTES

KEY VERSES

PRAYER

KEY POINTS

APPLICATION

# Prayer journal

DATE _____

TODAY'S PASSAGE          PREACHER          SERMON TOPIC

NOTES
_____
_____
_____
_____
_____
_____
_____
_____
_____
_____
_____
_____

PRAYER
_____
_____
_____
_____
_____
_____
_____
_____
_____
_____
_____
_____
_____
_____
_____
_____

KEY VERSES

KEY POINTS

APPLICATION

# Prayer journal

DATE _____

TODAY'S PASSAGE          PREACHER          SERMON TOPIC

NOTES
_____
_____
_____
_____
_____
_____
_____
_____
_____
_____
_____
_____

PRAYER
_____
_____
_____
_____
_____
_____
_____
_____
_____
_____
_____
_____
_____
_____
_____
_____
_____

KEY VERSES

KEY POINTS

APPLICATION

DATE _____

# *Prayer journal*

TODAY'S PASSAGE          PREACHER          SERMON TOPIC

NOTES
_____
_____
_____
_____
_____
_____
_____
_____
_____
_____
_____

PRAYER
_____
_____
_____
_____
_____
_____
_____
_____
_____
_____
_____
_____
_____
_____
_____

KEY VERSES

KEY POINTS

APPLICATION

DATE _____

# Prayer journal

TODAY'S PASSAGE          PREACHER          SERMON TOPIC

NOTES
_____
_____
_____
_____
_____
_____
_____
_____
_____
_____
_____
_____

| KEY VERSES |
| --- |
| |

PRAYER
_____
_____
_____
_____
_____
_____
_____
_____
_____
_____
_____
_____
_____
_____
_____
_____
_____

| KEY POINTS |
| --- |
| |

| APPLICATION |
| --- |
| |

# Prayer journal

DATE _____

TODAY'S PASSAGE          PREACHER          SERMON TOPIC

NOTES
_____
_____
_____
_____
_____
_____
_____
_____
_____
_____

| KEY VERSES |
| --- |
|  |

PRAYER
_____
_____
_____
_____
_____
_____

| KEY POINTS |
| --- |
|  |

_____
_____
_____
_____
_____
_____
_____
_____

| APPLICATION |
| --- |
|  |

# Prayer journal

DATE _____

TODAY'S PASSAGE         PREACHER               SERMON TOPIC

NOTES

_____

_____

_____

_____

_____

_____

_____

_____

_____

_____

_____

| KEY VERSES |
| --- |
| |

PRAYER

_____

_____

_____

_____

_____

_____

_____

| KEY POINTS |
| --- |
| |

_____

_____

_____

_____

_____

_____

_____

_____

_____

| APPLICATION |
| --- |
| |

DATE _____

# Prayer journal

TODAY'S PASSAGE          PREACHER          SERMON TOPIC

NOTES
_____

| KEY VERSES |
| --- |
| |

PRAYER
_____

| KEY POINTS |
| --- |
| |

| APPLICATION |
| --- |
| |

# Prayer journal

DATE

TODAY'S PASSAGE          PREACHER          SERMON TOPIC

NOTES

KEY VERSES

PRAYER

KEY POINTS

APPLICATION

# Prayer journal

DATE _____

TODAY'S PASSAGE          PREACHER          SERMON TOPIC

NOTES
_____
_____
_____
_____
_____
_____
_____
_____
_____
_____
_____

| KEY VERSES |
| --- |
| |

PRAYER
_____
_____
_____
_____
_____
_____
_____
_____
_____
_____
_____
_____
_____
_____
_____
_____

| KEY POINTS |
| --- |
| |

| APPLICATION |
| --- |
| |

# Prayer journal

DATE

TODAY'S PASSAGE         PREACHER         SERMON TOPIC

NOTES

KEY VERSES

PRAYER

KEY POINTS

APPLICATION

# Prayer journal

DATE _____

TODAY'S PASSAGE          PREACHER          SERMON TOPIC

NOTES
_____
_____
_____
_____
_____
_____
_____
_____
_____
_____
_____

PRAYER
_____
_____
_____
_____
_____
_____
_____
_____
_____
_____
_____
_____
_____
_____
_____

KEY VERSES

KEY POINTS

APPLICATION

DATE _____

# Prayer journal

TODAY'S PASSAGE          PREACHER          SERMON TOPIC

NOTES
_____

KEY VERSES

PRAYER
_____

KEY POINTS

APPLICATION

# Prayer journal

DATE _____

TODAY'S PASSAGE　　　　PREACHER　　　　SERMON TOPIC

NOTES
_____
_____
_____
_____
_____
_____
_____
_____
_____
_____
_____

| KEY VERSES |
| --- |
| |

PRAYER
_____
_____
_____
_____
_____
_____
_____
_____
_____
_____
_____
_____
_____
_____
_____
_____

| KEY POINTS |
| --- |
| |

| APPLICATION |
| --- |
| |

DATE _____

# Prayer journal

TODAY'S PASSAGE       PREACHER       SERMON TOPIC

NOTES

_____

_____

_____

_____

_____

_____

_____

_____

_____

_____

_____

| KEY VERSES |
| --- |
| |

PRAYER

_____

_____

_____

_____

_____

_____

_____

| KEY POINTS |
| --- |
| |

_____

_____

_____

_____

_____

_____

_____

_____

_____

| APPLICATION |
| --- |
| |

DATE _____

# Prayer journal

TODAY'S PASSAGE          PREACHER          SERMON TOPIC

NOTES
_____

| KEY VERSES |
| --- |
|  |

PRAYER
_____

| KEY POINTS |
| --- |
|  |

| APPLICATION |
| --- |
|  |

Made in United States
North Haven, CT
09 November 2022

26451956R00090